C000150207

EXMOOR WALKS FROM MINEHEAD

EXMOOR WALKS

from Minehead

BRIAN ATKIN

Illustrated by the Author

EXMOOR BOOKS
in association with
Exmoor Tourist Association

First published in 1998 by Exmoor Books
Copyright © 1998 A.B. Atkin

*All rights reserved. No part of this publication may
be reproduced, stored in a retrieval system, or transmitted
in any form or by any means, electronic, photocopying, recording or
otherwise, without the prior permission of the publishers.*

ISBN 0 861834 35 6

British Library Cataloguing-in-Publication-Data
A CIP data for this book is available from the British Library

EXMOOR BOOKS
Dulverton, Somerset

Exmoor Books is a partnership between
The Exmoor Press and The Exmoor National Park Authority.

Trade sales enquiries
HALSGROVE
Halsgrove House
Lower Moor Way
Tiverton EX16 6SS
T: 01884 243242
F: 01884 243325
www.halsgrove.com

Printed and bound in Great Britain
by Hillman Printers (Frome) Ltd

FOREWORD

The Exmoor Tourist Association is delighted to be associated with this publication. The Association is very grateful to local author Brian Atkin both for writing this book and for recognizing the need for a new walking publication covering the Minehead area.

Minehead is surrounded by some of the finest walking country in England. It is also the starting point of the South West Coast Path, something travel writers so often forget. This book succeeds in proving that, whether you are a local or a visitor, you can spend two wonderful weeks on walks from Minehead without using a car.

The Association is delighted that the author will be giving all royalties from this book to the Exmoor Paths Partnership. This excellent group seeks continually to improve and protect the myriad paths across Exmoor for future generations to enjoy.

The Association is very grateful to the following groups and individuals for their commitment to and support of this project: Richard Partington at Exmoor National Park; Mandy Berry at the Greater Exmoor LEADER Project; Steven Pugsley at Exmoor Books; Tim King, the Tourism Officer for West Somerset District Council; the Minehead Hotels Association, and the Minehead Development Forum. Without their valuable support this most worthwhile project would not have been achieved.

Michael Simons,
Chairman,
Exmoor Tourist Association

CONTENTS

INTRODUCTION

Exmoor, only 267 square miles in extent, is one of the smallest English National Parks. Yet this quiet and relatively unknown region contains some of the country's very best and most varied scenery.

Exmoor confronts the sea in an awesome line of hills and cliffs unequalled elsewhere in England. In between these rocky slopes mountainous streams tumble onto lonely stony beaches once frequented by smugglers. Inland the ancient rocks present a very different aspect. Here bottom lands are covered by small irregular fields carved from the wildwood long ago. Above them rise steep valley sides covered in native sessile oaks which in turn lead to stark high moors covered in heather and grass. On climbing away from the pretty flower gardens of old thatched cottages it does not take very long or far to reach an alien bleak world of bare windswept tops. Yet the whole of Exmoor has a sense of unity which even embraces recent man-made conifer forests.

The region's pervasive other-world charm has given rise to many stories and legends, of which R.D. Blackmore's novel *Lorna Doone* is the most famous. But away from Oare and Badgworthy Water there are numerous peaceful mysterious places and many are explored in this guide. Deep, tree-covered combes close in to form green-roofed naves where nothing breaks the silence but gurgling little streams in the bottom. Out on the empty tops sheep and whirling buzzards are often the only companions except for occasional red deer or semi-wild Exmoor ponies. Yet even up here man's past is evident in Bronze Age tumuli, eroded Iron Age fortifications, vestigial remains of former fields and some more recent scars of iron-ore mining.

To complement these scenic delights, the Exmoor National Park Authority maintains a bewildering choice of signposted and well-maintained paths which lead to every pleasure and corner of the region.

All the walks in this guide are based on Minehead, a bright and busy little seaside town and the natural capital of the region. It offers a wide range of holiday accommodation, restaurants, shops and all other essential facilities. The town is also the focal point for local public transport. Nearly surrounded by sea and National Park, Minehead makes an ideal place to explore the beautiful surrounding countryside.

This guide gives detailed route descriptions for five circular walks starting from Minehead and seven more energetic linear rambles back to the town using public transport. Taken together they can provide the basis for a fortnight's restful holiday with no driving and parking problems.

Winter sunshine and shadows along the shingle bank, Porlock Bay

The moors roll on and away to seeming infinity.

POINTS TO NOTE

- Although the route descriptions in the guide give all the necessary advice for those who want to follow the walks, a detailed map is often helpful and also provides additional fascinating information on the surroundings. The 1:25,000 Ordnance Survey Outdoor Leisure Map No. 9, covering the whole region, is the best buy for this purpose.

- Before setting off on any of the seven linear walks, it is important to check bus and train times as these may change from time to time. Timetables are available from the Tourist Information Centre and the station in Minehead.

- Exmoor may have a more kindly climate than other upland areas of Britain but this should never be taken for granted when venturing onto its lonely exposed places. Precautions for all Exmoor wild-country walks, especially when the weather is unreliable, include: a good pair of walking boots, raingear, spare warm clothes, a first aid kit, a compass, a map, food and drink, a whistle and a torch on short winter days. Finally, when arranging a lone walk, route details should always be left behind with a responsible person.

Considerable effort has been made to ensure the accuracy of the walk descriptions but the author cannot be held responsible if anyone comes to harm while following them.

Brian Atkin
Minehead, 1998

ACKNOWLEDGEMENTS

Many thanks to Sunya, Gavin, Carole, Matthew, Christopher, Katie and Ken, members of my family who meticulously checked the routes and descriptions, also to my friends Cyril Page and Malcolm Lawson for their companionship and helpful advice and finally to Malcolm Higgins for his untiring efforts to have the guide published.

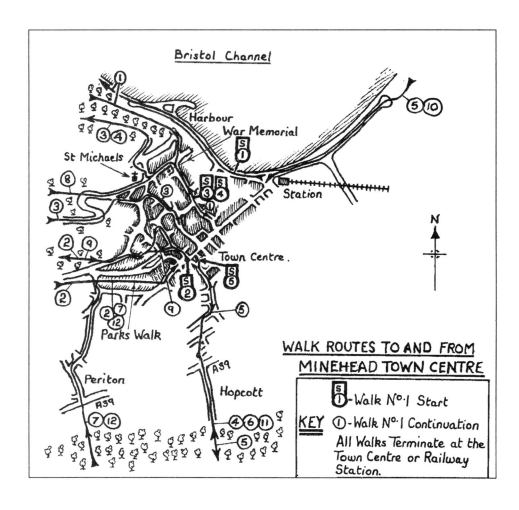

Bristol Channel

Harbour
War Memorial

St Michaels

Station

Town Centre.

Parks Walk

Periton

A39

Hopcott

N

WALK ROUTES TO AND FROM
MINEHEAD TOWN CENTRE

KEY

🅂① - Walk Nº·1 Start

① - Walk Nº·1 Continuation

All Walks Terminate at the
Town Centre or Railway
Station.

⇢ WALK 1 ⇠

WESTWARDS ALONG THE COAST
AND BACK OVER THE MOOR

Minehead Harbour, Culvercliff, Greenaleigh Farm and Burgundy Chapel, returning along the South West Coast Path. This 4-mile, two-hour saunter gives a first taste of the high wild lonely coast which stretches for 30 miles from Minehead to the west. There is one high, steep hill to climb.

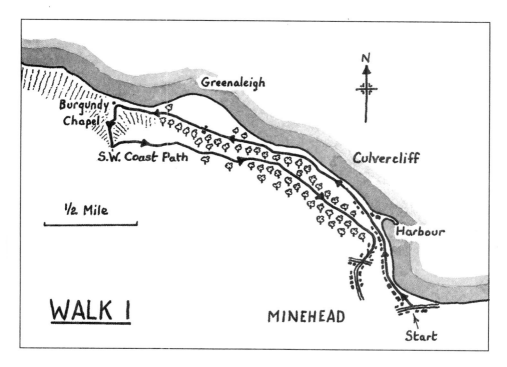

(1) The walk commences along the town centre Avenue to the sea front.

(2) A left turn at the Esplanade passes old cottages on the left and the harbour and lifeboat house on the right, eventually leading to the turning circle at the end of the road.

Minehead harbour

(3) With all buildings left behind, the route now follows a tarmac path along the edge of an open green space above the shingle shore and sea.

The new scene has two dominating features: on the left a high bank crowded with trees and on the right the empty waters of the Bristol Channel.

(4) At the end of the grassy area the path enters trees above the shore. The way forward now becomes steep and stony.

(5) Ignoring a path on the left, the route continues to climb in a more or less straight line, eventually joining a level track.

(6) On turning right this track soon narrows briefly at the site of an old landslide into the sea, presenting views over the water and a glimpse of the stony shore below.

(7) Further along this track joins the vehicle route to Greenaleigh Farm. Massed trees still continue on the left but farm meadows now appear on the right, sliding down towards the sea.

(8) At Greenaleigh the route continues straight ahead, with the house and outbuildings on the left and a barn on the right, aiming for the trees ahead. The signposted path on the right heading for the shore should be ignored. The dogs at the isolated farm may bark on approach but are basically friendly.

(9) The new path is less used. As it is periodically enclosed by overhanging bushes and then opens to vistas across the sea, progress is marked by contrasting intervals of intimacy and space.

In dry weather the one wet and muddy patch along the way has its origins in an ancient well set into the side of the hill.

(10) Beyond the spring the path veers inland to the site of Burgundy Chapel. This mysterious lonely ruin, all but hidden in wild undergrowth, is approached down steep steps. The information board makes fascinating reading. By now it is hard to appreciate that the busy town of Minehead is only 2 miles away.

(11) From here the path veers right and heads steeply inland up tall Burgundy Combe. This route is mountainous and as the top is far above there is no point in attempting to hurry.

(12) The view widens during the climb revealing steep hills on each side falling away into the sea far below. Two-thirds of the way up a wooden seat provides a good resting place.

A nearby hillock reveals the combe, the recently climbed path and the wide reaches of the Bristol Channel. It is a delightful spot to dally on a sunny summer's day.

(13) The final stage of the climb ends at a well-used track beside a signpost. This is the South West Coast Path and the turning point of the walk. The way ahead is not uphill towards Poole in Dorset, more than 600 footpath miles away, but to the left, contouring along the face of the hill back to Minehead.

There are now wide views over the Bristol Channel, its moods always mirroring those of the sky above. At first the way passes across moorland but on the gradual descent this gives way to bushes and then to tall trees which mask distant views.

(14) Eventually the vehicle track from Greenaleigh climbs to join the route. Soon the boundary sign of Exmoor National Park is passed and the rough walking surface changes to smooth tarmac. The way veers to the right.

Ahead a wayside seat comes into view. It commands an extensive view of Minehead Harbour, Minehead Bay, Blue Anchor Bay, the Quantocks, the islands of the Bristol Channel and, on fine clear days, the distant Mendips. This scene changes constantly with the state of tide, the time of day, the weather and the season and never fails to capture the eye.

(15) At the junction with Beacon Road the route abandons the coast path ,which continues down the steep zigzag path, taking instead a gentle downhill stroll along Burgundy Road to the War Memorial. From here Martlet Road leads back to the town centre.

$\rightarrow$ WALK 2 $\leftarrow$

AROUND THE HILLS AND ALONG
THE VALLEY BACK TO MINEHEAD

Whitecross Lane, Woodcombe, Bratton Ball, Bratton and the Bratton Walk. This walk passes through a peaceful quiet countryside of trees, moorland and meadows only a short step from the busy town centre. As the route is relatively low-lying and away from the exposed high coast, it is suitable for a wet-weather day. A three-hour, 4-mile ramble with modest hills to climb.

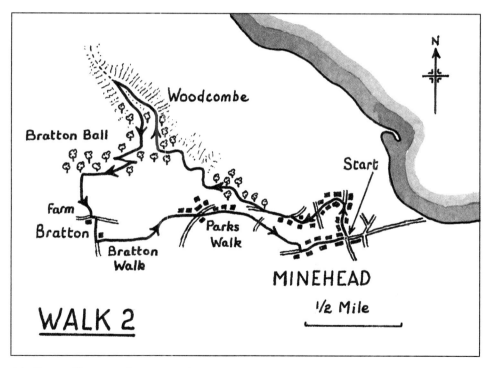

(1) The walk starts from Minehead town centre, going up Holloway Street.

(2) After passing old thatched cottages on the left, it turns left into Middle Street with the Adult Education Centre on the right.

(3) Beyond the narrow corner at the cottage known as Falkland Court, the steps on the right leading up and the entrance to Hemp Gardens should both be ignored. The next track on the right, heading past the end of a row of terraced houses, is the way to go.

(4) This soon dwindles to a path and then emerges onto the narrow lane known as Western Road.

(5) The way forward lies opposite and slightly downhill along a tarmac path which starts beside the bricked end of a tall stone wall between the drives of two properties.

(6) The new path briefly becomes a grassy track before reverting to tarmac. The downhill turning on the left should be ignored. At the end, a short, steep climb up a cul-de-sac leads to Whitecross Lane,where the route turns left.

(7) After 150 yards the walk heads onto a path veering right through bushes and trees. The entrance is marked by a prominent fire-warning notice.

(8) By now the buildings of the town have been left behind. However, as the path climbs slowly across the face of the steep wooded hillside there are occasional glimpses of houses below.

(9) The way continues ahead, ignoring side turnings to both right and left. At one point the path becomes a track and then reverts to a path again. All the time height is gradually being gained.

(10) The path eventually swings to the right and away from the town into the smaller of two combes. Moorland hillside is now in view ahead.

(11) After crossing the first combe and passing further along the side of the hill, the path drops down into the second, the much larger Woodcombe. At a T-junction in the bottom there is a broad and well-used track. Here the route turns right and up a stony, sometimes muddy surface. Trees close in as the only significant climb of the walk begins.

(12) The track rises up the combe parallel to an old boundary wall on the left. One hundred and fifty yards beyond a well-beaten path on the right there is another on the left. This is the way to go, heading back across the western side of the valley. The new path at first heads gently downhill and then becomes almost level.

Trees remain but it is now possible to peer down through foliage back to the ascending track in the combe bottom.

(13) At length the path follows the side of the hill out of the combe and onto a less steep hillside which overlooks the main valley containing Minehead.

(14) After crossing a stile, the only one on the route, the path turns left and down the face of the hill on a long zigzag through trees, eventually meeting a track at the bottom. Here the route turns right, passing along the uphill side of a hedgerow bordering fields in the valley bottom.

Through the hedge there are glimpses of these fields backed by high wooded hills and also the buildings of Bratton Court, a large old farm which is the next objective along the route.

(15) The way ahead now turns left through a large iron gate into an enclosed sunken track heading for the farm. At the lowest point, close to a small stream, the surface can be soft and muddy in wet weather.

(16) Immediately opposite the farm buildings, the track enters a narrow, metalled lane. Through the arch ahead it is possible to glimpse the fascinating medieval features of the old farmhouse.

(17) After turning left at the lane, there is an immediate turn to the right along another. This leads down to a small ford with a miniature footbridge. From here the remainder of the walk follows the stream back to Minehead.

(18) Just beyond the old thatched cottage on the left, the route turns left down a drive to a garage. The gate providing access to Bratton Walk is initially out of sight on the right.

(19) The way ahead is now well used, at first passing beside a lovely garden and then along field edges close to the valley bottom. Above, undulating meadows lead up to higher, wilder, wooded hills.

(20) The rural pleasures of the walk end shortly after crossing the stream. On reaching the houses and bungalows of suburban Woodcombe, the path enters a small, well-maintained park with a pond and decorative trees and then heads for the main road.

(21) Visibility is not good in either direction and the road crossing needs care. On entering Woodside Gardens, a tarmac footpath can be seen on the left of the stream. This is the start of the Parks Walk.

(22) The path beside the stream heads for a grassy recreational area, formerly a water meadow. On reaching the road at the end, the walk turns right and immediately left onto another path. This follows the stream for a short distance before cossing over and passing through an attractive formal garden.

(23) The final water crossing is near Parkhouse Road. From here a left turn leads to the nearby town centre. By this stage the stream is out of sight, running in a culvert beneath the highway.

⤞ WALK 3 ⤝

A HIGH LEVEL WALK AROUND NORTH HILL

Beacon Hill, North Hill and Woodcombe. This is an elevated walk with spectacular views over sea, coast and hills. It requires one long, gentle climb at the outset. Four miles and two hours of steady walking.

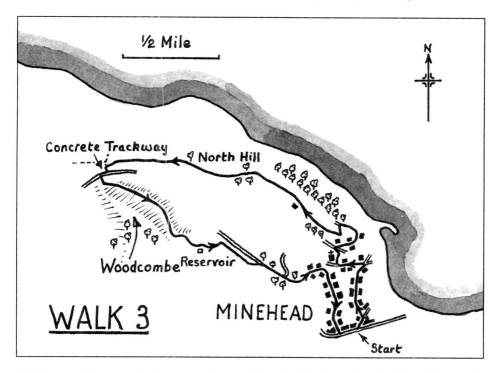

(1) The walk leaves the town centre up Martlet Road and at the War Memorial bears left towards St Michael's Church.

(2) Here it turns right up Church Road with the church on the left.

(3) Beyond the entrance to Cleveland Chalets, the way turns sharp left at the next gap and follows a grassy path up the slope past a seat before climbing a flight of steps up to Beacon Road.

(4) The climb continues as the route turns left and immediately right into North Hill Road, which is followed past scattered dwellings to its end high above the sea.

(5) Twenty yards in front of upright posts blocking further vehicular access, the walk turns left up a path signposted to North Hill. There is now an old stone-faced boundary bank on the left. On reaching a second well-used gap the route turns left entering trees, the less-frequented original path now being ignored.

(6) The new route wanders westwards through the trees until it encounters a wire fence on the edge of a high meadow. Here it turns left and downhill to a gate, stile and signpost at the lower corner of the field.

(7) After the stile the line of march veers right and uphill, crossing further stiles and heading for a gate in the hedgerow ahead. A distinctive clump of distant pines provides a useful waymark.

(8) Beyond the first gate there is another immediately on the right. After passing through both, the route follows an undulating path below a modern cowshed, and a further gate gives access to an elevated field with the pines at its far end.

Please remember to shut the gates behind you if you find them closed. Young cattle often inhabit these fields during the summer months (they never seem more than mildly curious of passers-by, however).

(9) After following the left side of the last field up to the pines it is time to look to the rear.

The nearby ground drops away over the fields back to Beacon Hill and beyond the West Somerset coast extends towards the lonely Quantock Hills. Below on the left the sea can be as blue as the Mediterranean on fine sunny days, contrasting sharply with the mysterious, tree-covered hills straddling the horizon on the right.

(10) The route leaves the field over a stile between two field gates and then enters tall scrub where distant views are restricted. The path proceeds straight ahead, westwards and upwards beside an old boundary bank. Other paths to the right and left should all be ignored. On encountering a well-used cross path, the route turns sharp right and immediately left, to continue on beside the boundary bank.

(11) Trees and bushes are left behind as the walk reaches the open space of the moor which provides a riot of colour in high summer.

On the edge of the moor an old concrete trackway crosses the line of march. This is one of several wartime features in the area that are now merging back into the landscape. They date from the time before D-Day when this moor was used for battle training.

The climb has now ended. There are splendid views, to the Bristol Channel on one side and, on the other, to wooded hills which will be traversed on later walks. In addition a new feature has appeared: heather-clad Dunkery Beacon. This, the highest hill on Exmoor, soon disappears behind the nearby bulk of Bratton Ball but will return to view later from the high path above Woodcombe.

(12) The present track is broad and runs parallel to the road on the left. Further along the route branches left at a fork. On reaching a small parking area the way ahead is left onto the road, which is followed to the right and westwards for a short distance. A footpath signposted to Woodcombe appears on the left and this leads into the upper reaches of the Woodcombe valley.

(13) During the descent, the first path junction on the right provides a waymark. One hundred and fifty yards further down, the walk turns left onto a path heading upwards. After 30 yards the way forward turns right along a delightful high, level path which contours across the steep east slope of Woodcombe.

This open hillside presents lovely views which encompass the deep valley below, the wooded bank opposite and distant hills including Dunkery Beacon.

(14) As the path leaves the combe for the hillside above the town, there is a wide view over the clustered buildings down to the sea beyond.

(15) At a meeting of tracks close to a covered reservoir, the walk crosses over and heads uphill.

(16) The road along the moor, now on its descent, comes into view on the left and the way ahead is along a downhill track on its right. This track eventually joins the highway.

During the descent the surrounding vegetation changes from spartan moor to lush woodland and soon full-grown trees press in on all sides.

(17) Just before the road takes a sharp left bend, there is a wooden seat, also on the left. The walk follows a narrow path to the left of the seat which leads back to the road below the hairpin bend. On reaching the tarmac once more, the way ahead can be seen slightly uphill across the road. This new path heads away through trees.

Church Steps, Minehead

These trees soon give way to steep meadows falling into a combe, presenting a panoramic view of the upper part of Minehead with the sea beyond. These homes, overlooked by the parish church, are known as Higher Town. They are protected by the surrounding hills from all but the chill east wind which on occasion roars in from the open water.

(18) The final section of path curves down to Moor Road. Here the route turns right and then left into Vicarage Road, where the famous old cottages flanking Church Steps come into view.

(19) The walk continues around into Church Street and then into Holloway Street back down to the town centre.

⇢ WALK 4 ⇠

A WESTERN CIRCUIT OF MINEHEAD

Beacon Hill, the South West Coast Path, Selworthy, East Lynch, Headon Cross, Tivington Common and Wootton Common, returning to Minehead via Hopcott. This walk is a lovely combination of high and low level walking through woodland, farmland and across moors. The picturesque village of Selworthy is visited and there are frequent reminders of the nearby sea. Eight miles and five hours of steady walking with two substantial hills to climb.

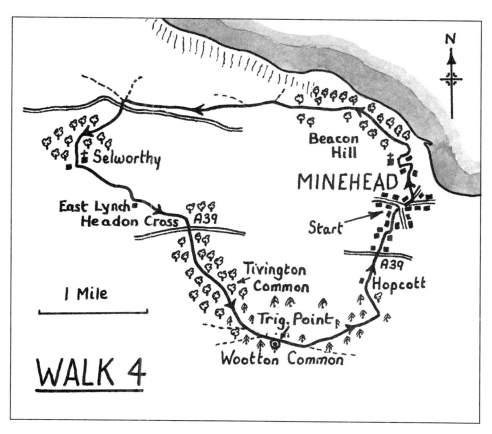

(1) The walk commences in the town centre, going up Martlet Road to the War Memorial and continuing on to St Michael's Church.

(2) In front of the church the route takes a right turn up Church Road.

(3) Ignoring the turning to Cleveland Chalets, the walk then takes the next opening on the left. Here a path on rising grassy ground leads past a seat to steps and Beacon Road.

(4) Turning left and then immediately right into North Hill Road, the route follows the tarmac all the way up and around scattered dwellings to its end above the sea.

(5) From here a near-level track continues westwards through tall mature trees. The path on the left followed in Walk 3 and all others should be ignored.

The present route is parallel to the almost identical Coast Path further down the hill.

(6) Eventually, after a steady climb, the trees begin to thin out to scrubland and an old wartime building is passed on the right. One hundred and fifty yards further on, after crossing a old concrete apron and passing a wooden seat, the route reaches open moorland.

Here, owing to the open terrain and falling ground on both sides, there is greater exposure to the weather of the day.

(7) At length the Coast Path climbs from the right to join the present route and the combined track continues on through gorse and heather with a view of the sea through Grexy Combe. The signposted Rugged Coastpath on the right should be ignored.

Ahead, moorland eventually gives way to meadows. There were two farms up here until the Second World War, when this plateau became a battle-training ground. Up to then there had been human occupation in the area for many centuries, as shown by the remains of the Iron Age fort on Furzebury Brake above Grexy Combe. Nowadays, apart from grazing cattle and sheep, this is a lonely part of the world.

(8) There is a hand gate where the Coast Path meets the corner of the meadows. Immediately beyond this spot the walk leaves the Coast Path for another track closer to the road on the left. This is reached by heading half left towards the gate on the right of a prominent road sign. The intervening ground is partly obstructed by clumps of thorny gorse.

(9) From the second gate onwards the new path is clear-cut across a gorsy moor, ignoring a diagonal track junction. After proceeding for three-quarters of a mile parallel to the road, the path reaches a T-junction with a tarmac-covered concrete trackway.

By now the scene ahead has undergone a radical change. Gently rising moorland has given way to a wide view of Selworthy Beacon, falling away to Selworthy Combe. The latter is the next objective. The route turns left for a short distance down to the road, crosses over, and joins a track. Fifty yards further on this is signposted to Selworthy and Dunster.

Deepening Selworthy Combe now lies on the right. As the valley descends, the moor first gives way to bushes, then to small trees and finally, near the bottom, to towering sweet chestnuts.

(10) The walk now takes the side turning on the right leading down into the shelter of this combe.

Ahead a small but prominent roof marks Lady Gertrude Acland's Hut. Although much modified since her day, it is still well worth visiting and, if needed, provides a place of refuge from the elements.

Lady Gertrude Acland's Hut, Selworthy Combe

Selworthy

(11) The track along the combe bottom is joined by another on the right and continues down through trees to Selworthy.

Few other people will have been seen over the preceding miles, but some will be evident now, whether it is in or out of season. This pretty village is one of the best-known tourist spots in England.

The path on the right beside the War Memorial leads down to the famous green and its picturesque cottages. During the holiday season there is also a welcome café/tea garden here and a shop.

Selworthy is often regarded as an unspoilt old English village, but this impression is false. The delightful thatched cottages, placed tastefully around the green, were extensively modified by the benevolent Aclands in the nine-teenth century, for retirement homes for their estate workers.

(12) The tempting paths leading away in all directions should be resisted. On returning uphill, the walk passes in front of the church, heading eastwards along a narrow lane.

(13) After half a mile there is a right turn onto an unsurfaced bridleway, which leads past an old thatched house on the left and then the buildings of East Lynch Farm on the right. The bridleway eventually becomes a metalled lane, is joined by another from the left, and descends below Little Headon Plantation to the main A39 road at Headon Cross.

This is the watershed between the Vale of Porlock and the valley leading down to Minehead. Significantly for walkers, it is also the saddle between the hills of the first half of the walk and those of the second.

(14) The tree-covered hillside directly ahead is the next objective. After crossing the busy main road, the route follows the lane opposite for a few steps before taking a bridleway on the left through trees.

(15) During the climb all other tracks and paths to both right and left should be ignored, even well-established forestry tracks. Higher up and beyond the National Trust boundary, old native woodland gives way to commercial forestry.

(16) On nearing the top of the ridge the track veers to the left and eastwards. All other tracks filtering in from both left and right should be ignored. It is now advisable to look at the hedge on the right for the concrete O.S. Point which marks the 295-metre spot height.

(17) From this waymark the walk continues for a quarter of a mile to the top of the next gentle rise before veering left along a track away from the ridgeway. This heads for Hopcott. After a descent through trees, a stretch of more open ground presents views of marshland and the sea.

(18) The route veers left at a fork and passes through more trees down to the top of the tarmac lane above Hopcott.

(19) On the way down the lane passes Higher Hopcott, the first house since East Lynch several miles back, and soon reaches the A39 on the edge of town.

(20) The route continues along a footpath between dwellings on the opposite side of the road, eventually ending on Poundfield Road where right and left turns onto Bampton Street lead down to the town centre.

Bampton Street was the original downtown Minehead and still contains a number of attractive old buildings.

➤ WALK 5 ➤

AN EASTERN CIRCUIT OF MINEHEAD

Hopcott, Grabbist Hill, Dunster, Dunster Marsh and back to Minehead along the beach. This is another walk of great interest and diversity, passing through woodland, traversing an airy ridge, visiting historic Dunster, crossing marshland and finally returning to Minehead across a sandy, stony shore. Seven miles and four hours of steady walking with one major hill to climb near the start.

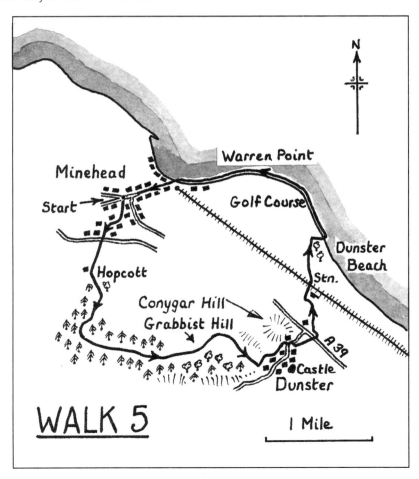

(1) This walk commences from Wellington Square at the top of the town centre.

(2) The route enters Bampton Street, next to the Wellington Hotel, and follows it left and uphill.

(3) At a corner food shop, the way ahead is right into Poundfield Road and, after 100 yards, left onto a pathway between buildings. This path continues in a more or less straight line, crossing Paganel Road and another short stretch of road before passing between more buildings up to the main A39 at Lower Hopcott.

(4) The lane opposite, on the right of a group of buildings, is then followed up to the top of the hills. Beyond Higher Hopcott with its lovely gardens, the route becomes steep and enclosed by trees.

(5) At the end of the tarmac, the walk takes the stony track on the right sign-posted to Timberscombe. The climb is now less steep.

In the new peaceful surroundings, the town already seems far away. At one point the view opens seaward, to the pincushion shape of Steep Holm and the headlands at Weston which masquerade as islands. Mysterious uninhabited Steep Holm always surprises by appearing in the most unexpected part of the scene.

(6) At a meeting of ways in front of tall trees, the route continues straight ahead.

(7) The flat top of the hill is marked by an open space with picnic seating. From here the route is left, following a well-used track along the ridge. Tempting deviations to both right and left should all be resisted.

Eventually sweeping views open out to the north, taking in Minehead with its many blue-slate and red-tiled roofs, the harbour full of boats and flat sea marshes to the east. During the past half century some of the watery green meadows have been covered with industrial buildings. On the right, wooded Conygar Hill, crowned by a folly, has now come into view.

(8) At length the track leaves the trees behind and enters lovely high open moorland. A fork to the right passes along the lip of the steep slope above the Avill Valley.

To the south the view stretches from meadows in the narrow bottom lands beside the river up to forested hills which culminate in the high tops of Croydon Hill and Withycombe Common. The continuing ridge, very colourful in late summer, falls gently eastwards towards the long undulating Quantock ridge. In the middle distance the attractive cliffs and beaches of the West Somerset coast contrast with the high stark coastline to the west of Minehead. This is a wonderful, airy place.

(9) Towards the end of Grabbist Hill, bushes and trees close in again. Side turns to the right and left should be ignored and eventually the track follows a wire fence on the left with trees on the right.

(10) At the end of the wire fence and above a pronounced slope, the route turns right onto a gently sloping path. From here are visible Conygar Hill and the castle, its romantic appeal heightened by Victorian mock-medieval battlements and towers, both overlooking the clustered buildings of Dunster.

(11) The route turns left above a cemetery, passes through a deer fence at a gate and then proceeds along a tarmac lane with allotments on the left. After a right turn, the lane continues down past a school to a road.

(12) The way forward is almost immediately opposite, along a lane with the churchyard on the right. Ahead an arch, marking the entrance to the medieval priory, stands close to an old restored dovecot and a tithe barn in need of repair.

(13) After passing under yet another arch, the lane continues along the back of the market-place buildings. Then a right turn leads to the classical view of Dunster, the yarn market, shops and buildings all dominated by the castle.

(14) The walk now turns left onto the main road through the village. The National Park Visitor Centre is on the right.

(15) Then the walk leaves Dunster. In the top corner of the car park, immediately below a large clothing store, there is a hand gate. This gives access to a public path across Dunster Park to Loxhole Bridge. Beyond this gate the path turns left across a grassy space.
  The clumps of trees and the green slopes of the park are backed by the red stone castle. This picturesque scene is sometimes complemented by gently grazing thoroughbred cattle.

(16) The exit from the park to the main road (the A39) is through a hand gate to the right of the vehicle entrance used by castle visitors. The road should be crossed with care.

(17) A field entrance opposite marks the start of the next path. With the

concrete-lined overflow channel of the Avill and the wood yard to the rear, the path initially follows the field side of the hedge bordering the main road and later turns along the side of the River Avill up to the lane leading to Dunster Beach.

Before the overflow channel was constructed this land was subject to periodic flooding, but now has several housing developments.

(18) On reaching the lane, the route turns left and immediately right to another lane heading down towards the shore. Nearby, a lovely disused bridge, apparently marooned in a private garden, should not be missed.

(19) The lane continues on past the railway station and the old manor house with its Gothic-windowed chapel above the front porch, then dwindles to a path on approaching a large, unattractive modern cowshed. After passing to the left of this building, the way forward is straight ahead across flat fields towards the level sea bank.

(20) Beyond a stone bridge over running water, the route turns right through bushes, passing a golf course on the left.

The stream drains the nearby marsh. On the right next to the sea bank, but hidden from view, there is a stretch of water known as the Hawn. It is believed to be the surviving remnant of Dunster's medieval harbour.

At the top of the sea wall, a bank composed of large rounded stones, can be seen a vast expanse of sea made finite by distant land features.

(21) From the bank top, the route is to the left. Sometimes the sea brushes the foot of the bank and at others it is far away across stony, sandy flats. There is a public footpath along the top of the sea bank back to Minehead but, if conditions allow, it is preferable to walk along the sand and stones to absorb the maritime scene without any distraction from activity on the golf course.

(22) From the beach, little can be seen of Minehead and its lovely hilly environs until the final bend at Warren Point is rounded.

(23) After passing the sea defences and Butlin's holiday centre, the railway station at the bottom of the town centre is soon reached.

⤜ WALK 5A ⤛

A GRAND CIRCUIT OF MINEHEAD

This walk circumnavigates Minehead, presenting a wide variety of scenery, ranging from a busy tourist resort to the lonely quiet of the hills and coast. The route is a combination of Walks 4 and 5. The description of Walk 4 is followed from item (1) to (16). Then, proceeding eastwards along the tree-covered ridge beyond Wootton Common, the route instructions beginning with item (7) of Walk 5 are followed back to Minehead. The walk is 12 miles long and requires a full day.

The beach and Beacon Hill, Minehead

⤃ WALK 6 ⤃

A WALK BACK TO MINEHEAD
FROM BLUE ANCHOR STATION

After a train journey from Minehead to Blue Anchor, the walk goes to Carhampton, Carhampton Gate, Withycombe Hill Gate, Bat's Castle, Dunster, Conduit Lane, Alcombe Common, Long Combe and finally through Hopcott back to Minehead. This attractive ramble passes through diverse scenery, including a sandy, stony shore, farmland, woods, moorland tops, an ancient hill fort, historic Dunster and a mixture of wild combes and hills. Predominantly peaceful scenes contrast with busy Dunster in high season. Eight miles and five hours of walking. There is one long hill to climb in the early stages and this is followed by a series of ups and downs over undulating terrain.

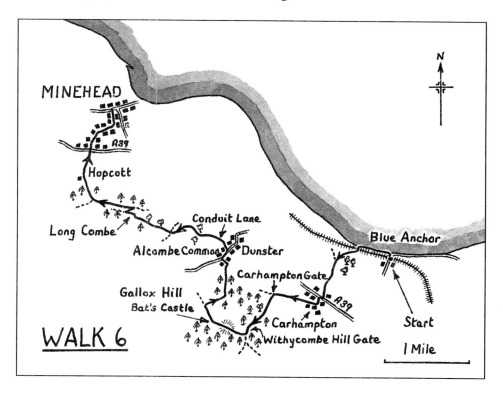

(1) On arriving at Blue Anchor station, the walker should turn right down the road to the nearby shore. From here the route turns left and back in the direction of Minehead along the public footpath which passes above the beach.

The name Blue Anchor is said to have originated in the days when sailing ships moored offshore. Their anchors when hauled up were covered with thick grey-blue mud formed from erosion of the lias cliffs to the east.

(2) The stony bank is heavy going, but the beach and the wide panorama provide compensation in full, especially when the tide is high. After a third of a mile and beyond the second railway signal on the left, the route joins a signposted public path over the rails.

(3) On the other side of the line the path crosses a stile, drops down and then heads half right over a flat meadow to the next stile adjacent to a field gate. The second meadow is then traversed to a third stile on the opposite side, close to the right-hand corner of a wood.

Once over the rails, the often noisy impact of the sea is abruptly replaced by quiet rural tranquillity.

(4) Veering left to the opposite corner of the third and largest meadow, the path

Across the fields to Carhampton

passes through a hand gate next to the sunken track known as Kitrow Lane, then follows it southwards along the field side of the bordering hedge. The stile on the right at Kitrow Lane should be ignored.

The ground starts to rise and undulate as the sea marshes are left behind. The village of Carhampton, identified by its prominent church tower, lies ahead.

(5) The path eventually joins the track, passes the church on the left and then reaches the A39, which runs through the village. The route now turns right, passes over the pedestrian crossing and then bears right and immediately left into the High Street.

Here a sign reading 'Carantoc Close' catches the eye. Carantoc is the Celtic saint to whom the parish church is dedicated and after whom the village is said to have been named. Carhampton, an old agricultural village, has in recent times become a pleasant residential centre.

(6) At the next T-junction in the village, the route turns right onto another lane. The houses are left behind and the tarmac surface eventually becomes a rough, stony track. All side turnings along the way should be ignored.

(7) On reaching the pronounced corner at Carhampton Gate, the entrance to Dunster deer park, the track turns sharp left and uphill. (For those wishing to shorten the walk, there is an opportunity to go directly to Dunster along the footpath through the deer park.)

The uphill continuation of Park Lane, a peaceful, tree-bordered track passing between farmland on one side and the deer park on the other, is the complete antithesis of its noisy, restless namesake in the West End of London.

(8) Higher up, woodland closes in. At the level top, there is a large wooden gate in the stone-faced boundary bank on the right. This is Withycombe Hill Gate. The route takes the walker through the gate and proceeds straight ahead along a level track through trees towards Bat's Castle.

(9) These trees soon end and moorland rises gently in front. The irregular winding earthwork that has appeared ahead was at one time thought to be a relic of the Civil War, during which nearby Dunster Castle was besieged more than once, but it is now associated with the impressive circular Iron Age hill fort on the crest of the slope ahead. This is Bat's Castle, a very exposed place in winter and a most uncomfortable one for the former inhabitants. No doubt they lived there only out of dire necessity.

From here a wide panorama of the hills ahead includes the lovely heathery slopes of Dunkery Beacon in the distance.

Bat's Castle with Dunkery in the distance

(10) On leaving the summit the path continues down to a saddle with Gallox Hill. This name sounds pleasant enough but is in fact a corruption of 'gallows hill'. Dunster's dreaded place of public execution once stood either here or at Gallox Bridge.

(11) The route does not ascend Gallox Hill but instead turns right into a tree-filled combe and goes all the way down to the bottom of the hill. Here it passes through a gate and, 100 yards further on, over a stile. The path descending from the right should be ignored. The way ahead is now right onto a track, then past some picturesque old cottages to reach the River Avill.

(12) Crossing the water via the old packhorse Gallox Bridge, the walker now approaches the busy centre of Dunster.

(13) After a short step up the lane, passing more old cottages, the route turns right up a footpath between buildings, heading straight towards a high, steep,tree-covered hill. This eminence was once crowned by the stone keep of the original Norman castle, demolished by the government at the end of the Civil War.

(14) On reaching the foot of this hill, the way turns left up a lane beside the mill

Gallox Bridge, Dunster

leat, to a right turn onto the main road through the village.

If the outing started with the first morning train from Minehead, it will now be lunchtime. In the summer months numerous different eating-places are open in Dunster, but out of season the choice is limited.

(15) Immediately after an old Nonconformist chapel on the left, now converted into a tourist shop, the walk turns left into St George's Street. Beyond the school the road reaches an area of substantial stone houses. Here, next to the sign at the entrance to Hangars Lane, the route turns left onto the unpaved Conduit Lane. Passing through fields, this heads westwards, up and away from the village.

(16) The track is often muddy, owing to water spilling from St Leonard's Well below the wooded hills ahead.

(17) Near the top of the fields the lane passes through a gate in a deer fence and the route turns right through trees.

(18) Three hundred yards ahead, after some smaller paths on the left (which should be ignored), there is a definite fork and the way turns left, climbing through conifer trees and eventually reaching a gate which gives access to scrubland.

This is the most peaceful and traffic-free way back to the centre of Minehead, but for the next mile or so it crosses the grain of the country ahead. Not only are there frequent ups and downs, but the wayfinding also needs care. If the route is lost, it is best to stay in the woodland but remain close to the meadows below.

(19) The path along the scrubland follows a wire fence for 300 yards before a right turn onto a pronounced downhill track. Then, almost immediately, the route turns left through a gate at a fork.

At this stage paths or tracks signposted to Alcombe or the Youth Hostel should be followed. Those to Ellicombe, and a downhill cross track, should be ignored.

The walk now passes through peaceful native woodland full of birches and oaks.

St Leonard's Well, Conduit Lane, Dunster

(20) Further along there are glimpses of meadows on the right and a signpost beside the path indicates that the Youth Hostel is close by. From here the route continues ahead and down into the bottom of the combe below Aldersmead.

(21) At the tarmac lane, the route turns right down to the stream, and then left onto the stony track up Long Combe. Several Exmoor combes share its name, but this combe is exceptional in being short.

Although by now Minehead is less than a mile away, this is a remarkably peaceful and sylvan setting.

(22) After climbing for a third of a mile beside the small stream in the valley bottom, the route turns right up a track doubling back through conifers along the north side of the combe.

(23) On reaching a T-junction the way turns left and up through trees beside a tall, ragged hedge bordering open meadows. This hedge is followed round to the right as the ground levels and then drops away. Further along, a fork to the left should be ignored.

(24) The track, still following the edge of the meadows, now drops down the hill. After a branch track which enters from the left (to be ignored), it passes through scrubland before dropping beneath more trees to the top of tarmac-covered Hopcott Lane. This descends past Higher Hopcott to the A39.

(25) Following the route taken in Walk 4, the walk crosses the road to the footpath between dwellings down to Poundfield Road.

(26) Here it turns right and then left into Bampton Street, which is then followed down to the town centre.

—◆—

⇥ WALK 7 ⇤

ALONG THE VALE OF PORLOCK
AND OVER WOOTTON COMMON

Starting from Porlock, the walk passes through Horner, Chapel Cross, Luccombe, Brockwell and Wootton Courtenay before climbing over Wootton Common to Periton and Minehead. The delightful Vale of Porlock, with high hills all around and glimpses of the sea in the distance, is followed by a steep ascent over Wootton Common to Minehead. Eight miles and four hours of brisk walking across undulating country with one tall hill near the end. The route is sheltered for most of the way and consequently suitable for wet-weather days. However, enjoyment will be infinitely greater on fine ones.

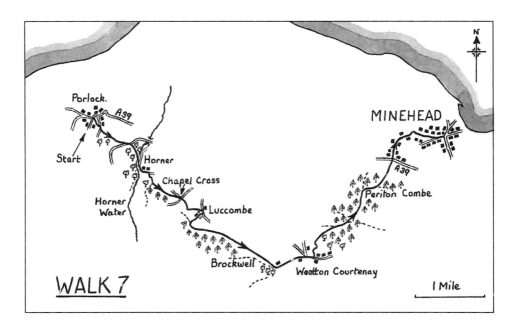

(1) The first stage of the journey is by the No. 38 bus from Minehead to Porlock, alighting at the parish church.

44

(2) The walk starts along a tarmac footpath to the left of the churchyard gates. Before heading away, it is worth taking a look at the church. Two unusual features immediately catch the eye: the truncated spire and the massively built tower below. The latter is the equal of anything found in castles and was probably built with protection from sea raiders in mind. This building is dedicated to another missionary of the early Celtic Church, St Dubricious (an unfortunate-sounding name, with its overtones of 'dubious', 'duplicitous' and 'suspicious'!).

(3) The broad tarmac footpath known as the Drang wanders past old and new dwellings, turns right at a fork and then passes through a kissing gate before going up a lane called Doverhay.

(4) Outside the village, at the first fork in the lane, the way ahead turns left towards West Luccombe and continues uphill for some distance.

(5) On reaching the eventual descent and just beyond the branch lane on the right heading towards Ley Hill, the walk turns right onto a bridleway. This is the lower of two paths: the higher one, known as Granny's Ride, should be ignored. The route now leads down through trees towards Horner.

There are meadows on the left, and then a campsite, one of the few within the National Park. Gaps in foliage reveal the green, rolling countryside of the Vale of Porlock leading up to high hills with glimpses of the sea beyond. For some distance, Selworthy's white church remains a prominent, eye-catching feature.

(6) The bridleway eventually reaches a point above Horner Water and later crosses the river by a tall, graceful packhorse bridge. At the lane on the other side, the walker will see a left turn leading to the car park and toilets and a right turn to a number of stone houses with tiled roofs.

Horner has two teashops and in modern times has become a popular starting point for the many beautiful walks nearby. It takes its name from the river: *horner*, which means 'snorer' in the old Celtic language, evokes the sound of waters in full spate.

(7) The walk continues along the lane towards Luccombe for a short distance. Immediately beyond the old water mill, now converted into a dwelling, the route leaves the road for an ascending track through trees on the right. The branch on the right behind the mill should be ignored. After a short climb the walk turns left at a fork and passes straight ahead along a gently ascending track through trees. At another fork the way ahead is again left, following the boundary with the fields below.

The rolling fields on the left, descending into the upper Vale of Porlock, were claimed for farmland long ago, but the rising, tree-covered ground on the right has remained in a semi-wild state. The impression of walking along the boundary between civilization and wilderness is heightened by knowledge that the open, heathery expanse of Dunkery stands above the trees.

(8) After half a mile the track passes through a gate onto a lane and the route turns right.

Before moving on it is worth while looking at the wide green verge on the opposite side of the lane, where the vestiges of a building can be seen. Apart from the fact that it was once a wayside chapel dedicated to St Anne, very little is known about it. Nevertheless, the memory of the place is preserved in the names of the nearby crossroads, Chapel Cross, and Chapel Steep, the road which climbs the hill above.

(9) The walk now heads over the crossroads along the narrow lane towards Luccombe. Some 200 yards further on, at a sharp bend to the left, it leaves the road for a winding, hedge-enclosed path on the right.

This is a rare path, the stuff of dreams. The closely mown turf provides a perfect cushion for the feet and no prickly fronds reach out from the well-tended wayside hedges to ensnare walkers' clothing.

(10) Eventually a hand gate appears on the left and the route turns into Luccombe churchyard.

The tall, slender tower of the church dominates the scene. The interior of the building is well worth exploring, not least for the brass plate in the floor below the altar which shows a William Harrison in Tudor clothing with a large, most uncomfortable-looking ruff around his neck. Outside, a pedestal and stump are all that remain of the cross said to have been destroyed by Parliamentarian troops during the Civil War.

Luccombe is a delightful, well-cared-for village with a balanced mix of old and new properties. The name of the place signifies 'an enclosed valley', and is still appropriate because the church and dwellings remain hidden away behind nearby hillocks.

(11) After passing through the lych-gate, the route turns right and southwards along Stoney Street, which belies its name with a modern covering of smooth tarmac.

(12) Beyond the final dwellings the route passes through a gate and turns left along a track over a bridge, with some trees and farmland on the left and higher, tree-covered ground on the right. This is a continuation of the track followed

earlier from Horner. There are several alternative ways forward but the route always follows the most obvious one. Even this can be muddy in places during wet weather. At a crossing of tracks further on, the way ahead is signposted to Brockwell.

(13) Soon afterwards the scene on the right reveals open moorland slopes above partly wooded enclosures.

Some of the latter, now a nature reserve, were once vegetable gardens. These were reclaimed from moorland during the nineteenth century to provide food for the many poor and hungry local inhabitants of the time. The land was last cultivated in the 1920s and has since reverted to a semi-wilderness where nature has prospered.

(14) It is worth walking through the first garden behind the nature reserve sign and afterwards turning left to return to the main track.

(15) In places the track is rough and irregular, but on approaching the tiny hamlet of Brockwell it becomes straight and true.

These surroundings were not always as quiet and peaceful as they are today. During the nineteenth century packhorses and wagons trundled past, carrying iron ore from the pits at Brockwell down to the sea at Porlock Weir for shipment to the blast furnaces of South Wales.

(16) At Brockwell the route skirts the scattered buildings and turns left onto the lane to Wootton Courtenay.

(17) Half a mile further on, after passing occasional large houses surrounded by meadows, the lane reaches the road through the village.

At this point it is pleasant to look back through a field gate at Robin How, the high eastern flank of the Dunkery range, which can be enjoyed at first hand on Walk 12.

(18) On joining the village road, the route turns right and, after 150 yards, left up a track that goes past the wooden village hall. This is Roadway Lane. Soon becoming steep, sunken, winding and hedge-enclosed, it runs up to the top of the tall hill ahead. Along the way there are few distant views to reward the walker and near the top trees crowd in on all sides.

(19) Here there is a multiplicity of tracks and paths. Fortunately an opportune sign beside the way points to Dunster and Periton and this should be followed.

(20) Eventually the route joins the track along the top of the ridge followed in Walk 4.

Distant views have now opened up towards Selworthy on the left, North Hill in front and a long panorama of the Welsh coast and hills across the sea.

(21) The route turns right and follows the ridge track eastwards for a short distance before turning left along a path across heathland signposted to Periton Combe.

(22) The descent of the ridge's northern side begins immediately and becomes steeper on entering the woods below. Again, with a choice of ways forward, the route is not always clear. However, as the next objective, Periton Combe, lies below and to the right of front, and there are also some helpful blue way-markers, there should be no problem.

(23) Eventually a twisting, well-used track leads to the bottom of the combe, where it is joined by another, and by a small stream which continues beside the way to the edge of the town.

(24) Soon after meadows appear on the left, the track reaches the A39 at a rather hazardous dip and bend. The road should be crossed with caution.

(25) The way ahead is now left into Periton Lane and then gently downhill through a mixture of old and new properties.

Periton was once a small hamlet quite separate from Minehead, but it has become absorbed into the growing town during the twentieth century.

(26) At a road junction, the continuation of Periton Lane begins at a dark, tree-enclosed gap flanked by vehicle no entry signs

Down in the hollow way shrouded by trees it is easy to imagine that meadows and fields still stand on both sides. For a while, all sounds of modern urban life are distanced and dulled, encouraging thoughts of old rural days and ways.

(27) At the end of the tunnel, Hillview Road, a modern suburban highway, passes downhill and veers left. A short distance down this road a tarmac path on the right, flanked by grass verges, marks the entry to the lower section of the Parks Walk.

(28) This leads through ornamental gardens to Parkhouse Road, where the route turns left and back to the town centre.

⇥ WALK 8 ⇤

ALONG A HIGH, WILD COAST

*Starting from Porlock, the route passes through Bossington, Hurlstone
Combe and along the Rugged Coastpath back to North Hill and Minehead.
Boots are essential for the rough walking conditions. There is one major hill
to climb, followed by less demanding ups and downs. Although not
vertiginous, the Rugged Coastpath should definitely be avoided in wild
weather. Eight miles and five hours of continuous walking.*

The walk was originally intended to begin at Porlock Weir. However, in
both subtle and dramatic ways, nature is always at work. A single stormy
tide in October 1996 destroyed the western end of the shingle bank across
Porlock Bay, scattering the stones inland and creating a major breach
through which subsequent tides have ebbed and flowed.

As a result, a popular section of the South West Coast Path has been
lost and at times the breach now becomes an impassable mass of raging
white water. Perhaps at some future date nature will permit a new path
across the bay, but for the time being the walk begins at Porlock village.
After crossing the fields and meadows of Porlock Vale, the new route joins
the old at Bossington and then mounts the high coast to the east. Even in
its modified form it is far too good to miss.

The shingle bank, Porlock Bay

(1) The expedition starts with a journey by No. 38 bus from Minehead to Porlock, where the walker should alight at the church.

(2) The route heads back along the village street for a few yards before turning left into Sparkhayes Lane next to the Countryman Restaurant.

(3) After 150 yards it turns right up concrete steps to a small estate of bungalows. At the entrance to the estate a left turn onto a lane leads northwards past houses and bungalows. The lane eventually turns left into Bay Road and here the walk takes a signposted, hedge-enclosed path to the right of front. This passes through fields with views across the marsh and shore.

(4) A left branch of the path heading straight ahead down to the shore should be ignored. Beyond the enclosing hedges the way passes through the first of two kissing gates and along the side of two fields to reach the second, where it turns left along another field edge.

These fields, famous for their high-quality barley, are much revered by beer drinkers.

High hills are now directly ahead, seemingly growing bigger every minute. The walk will soon climb to their tops.

(5) Beyond the second kissing gate the path goes along beside two fields before bearing left into another hedge-enclosed track. This winds past fields towards Bossington.

(6) Next, left and right turns around a farmhouse lead onto the village street. Here the route turns right.

Bossington is a National Trust village of old thatched and tiled dwellings. The massive stone chimney bases projecting into the street are a special attraction. These homes were originally built in the days when the smoke from open hearths was allowed to drift up into the sky through the thatch. It is said that when the new-fangled chimneys first came in, the well-to-do householders made this ostentatious display to engender envy among their less fortunate neighbours.

(7) Bossington has tea gardens, a car park and public toilets. There are no other such facilities between here and Minehead.

(8) Immediately beyond a cottage on the left which has a surprising Swiss-chalet style balcony on its flank, the route turns left beside the car park and over the river away from the village.

A corner of Bossington

(9) On the other side of the water, the track turns left through trees for a quarter of a mile, heading towards Hurlstone Point. Potential left turns along the way should be ignored; the walk continues ahead, passing through a gate.

On the left there are glimpses of meadows sliding down to the shore and on the right the high flank of Bossington Hill looms above. Very soon the walk will attain an even greater height.

(10) On reaching open ground, with the remains of the old lookout station and the crags of Hurlstone Point ahead, the route turns right up Hurlstone Combe. The long climb is best tackled slowly to avoid breathlessness.

During the climb, the gorse bushes and bracken in the valley bottom give way to large areas of scree precariously colonized by occasional small clumps of heather. For the first time on the walk, the mountainous features of Exmoor's coast become apparent.

(11) Close to the top there is a seat beside a meeting of ways. If the weather is fine this is a good place to take a breather.

(12) The path on the right should be ignored and so should the one with an admonitory notice on the left. The way forward is along a second path on the left, heading uphill, a few steps further up the hill.

This is the decision point of the walk. If the weather has deteriorated and the wind grown strong, it may be prudent to continue on to Minehead along the safe, well-signposted but much less attractive official South West Coast Path.

(13) Before long this second path on the left meets another running gently down towards the top of Hurlstone Point. This is the way to go.

From here on a clear day the famous high coastline can be seen marching away to the west. The long, gentle inland outlines of the moors turn abruptly into a succession of steep slopes which end in cliffs above the shore, a pattern repeated along the length of the Exmoor coast. It seems that there were once massive sea cliffs here which were ground down during the Ice Ages to their present smooth, steep, slanting profiles. In geological terms the sea has only recently returned, and so far has done no more than nibble away at their bases.

(14) Further down the slope, the route turns right at a fork, ignoring the path on the left continuing down to Hurlstone Point, and then climbs over the top of a small rise before turning east along the top of the seaward slope in the direction of East Combe.

Below the path there are signs of a massive landslide which has halted partway down and is now covered with coarse grass. Far below, tidal currents surge around Hurlstone Point, leaving Selworthy Sands with pock-marked patterns at low tide. This is a favourite place for fishing boats, as the swirling waters are rich feeding grounds for fish.

(15) The route now turns into East Combe and away from the sea. At a fork it veers left, leading down to a gate near the head of the valley. Although the path is an obvious one, very few people will be encountered over the next 3 miles.

The massive east bank of East Combe, falling away into the sea, is now in full view. Dense bracken in the upper reaches gives way to large sterile areas of scree towards the sea. With little to indicate scale, this valley and its hillsides seem much larger than they really are.

(16) The gate near the top of East Combe marks the start of the Rugged Coast-path. This name is a misnomer; only the surface of the path is rough, but a short distance away on the left there is a steep, 200-metre drop down to the sea.

(17) The path passes over hillocks at the head of East Combe and then climbs the opposite bank of the valley towards the sea.

(18) On reaching the top, it immediately heads south and down into the next valley, known as Henner's Combe.

(19) Two small streams are crossed near the valley head and the path climbs the east bank of Henner's Combe, heading once more towards the sea.

(20) Then, at a spot high above the water, the path turns right and follows the top of the elevated coast.

By now the shore and sea are far below, but the distant sound of waves provides a constant reminder of their presence.

(21) The path wanders up and down, close to the final boundary of the farm-land above.

Ragged dead pines stand against the sky at the site of the former West Myne farm. The spring which once met the needs of the former inhabitants and their animals still flows down across the path, creating a muddy patch in all seasons.

(22) Further along, the path crosses rocky ground at the site of old landslips. These are the Eastern Brockholes, presumably named after the badgers that made this unstable sanctuary their own.

At another spot, where the high coast continuing to the east first comes into view, there are several small rowans. They not only provide foraging sheep with shelter from the summer sun, but also present dazzling displays of orange-red berries each autumn.

(23) The high path above the sea comes to an abrupt end at the entrance to Grexy Combe. If the weather is fine this is an excellent spot to sit and enjoy the deep view embracing the valley, sea and surrounding hills.

(24) The path now leads into the combe away from the sea. There are two small streams to cross at the bottom, followed by a climb up the eastern flank before the route enters a side valley. The way forward is not always obvious, but helpful wooden posts provide a guide.

Around June, the whole of the valley bottom is covered with fragile flowering orchids, contrasting with the pervasive harshness of the scene.

(25) If all the ups and downs have become wearisome, it may be comforting to know that this is the last climb of the walk.

(26) At the top of the hill a fence, stile and meeting of tracks mark the end of the Rugged Coastpath. The way forward is along the path which proceeds straight ahead and eastwards across the top of the moor.

The nearby vestiges of earthen boundary banks date from the time when there was farmland up here.

(27) On reaching a track at a T-junction on the open moor, the route turns right. This track eventually veers left and up to a junction with the South West Coast Path, where the walk turns left, heading for Minehead.

(28) After a quarter of a mile across the top of the moor a junction of tracks is marked by a seat. This is where the South West Coast Path turns left and downhill, but the walk continues straight on, heading for the trees on the skyline.

(29) On arriving at these trees, it keeps going straight ahead, ignoring paths to both right and left, and soon reaches an old wartime concrete track. This continues gently downhill in the same direction as before. Again, all other turnings should be ignored.

(30) Immediately after an old vehicle loading ramp on the left, the route drops from the right-hand corner of the concrete onto a rough stony track. This is very soon joined from the left by a well-used farm track. Fifteen yards beyond this junction, a signposted path heads down a deepening combe on the left. This is the way to go.

To the east distant Blue Anchor Bay and the Quantocks have now come into view.

(31) The remainder of the route is downhill, at first heading for some groups of very tall pine trees. Although it is not obvious at this stage, the lower reaches of this combe shelter Minehead's Higher Town.

(32) A hundred yards below a small brick building, the route turns right onto a path which proceeds down through stately pines before passing along the right side of a long, narrow, sloping meadow in the valley bottom.

(33) On rejoining the track, the walk passes onto the road beside the first inhabited house since leaving Bossington 6 miles back.

(34) The route turns left, passing more homes and the church before reaching the War Memorial, where a right turn down Martlet Road leads back to the town centre.

⤛ WALK 9 ⤜

ACROSS THE HOLNICOTE ESTATE
TO MINEHEAD

*Starting from Allerford, the walk goes to Lynch Combe, the Memorial
Hut, Bury Castle, Selworthy, Dean's Cross, Bratton and Woodcombe
back to Minehead.*

*From a wooded hillside the walk mounts an airy ridge to visit the
Memorial Hut. Then, after wandering over lovely parkland to the Iron
Age fort of Bury Castle, the route passes through Selworthy. Finally a
ramble across tranquil farmland leads down the valley to Minehead.
Seven miles and five hours of steady walking with one steep hill to climb
near the start.*

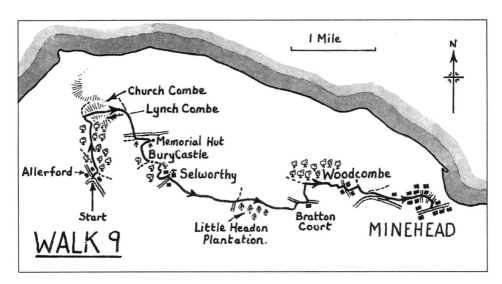

(1) The outing commences with a journey on the No. 38 bus from Minehead to
Allerford.

(2) From the bus stop, the route turns back towards Allerford; the main road
should be crossed with care. Then the way forward is down the lane on the left
to Allerford's packhorse bridge.

Allerford may not be as attractive as neighbouring Bossington or Selworthy, but it does have this gem of a bridge, and also a fascinating rural museum in the old school.

(3) The route crosses the little bridge and turns left onto a footpath signposted to Bossington. This rises up through a meadow before entering trees, the first of many on the high bank above.

(4) The path climbs gently and straight ahead for some distance. All other tracks and paths through the surrounding trees should be ignored.

(5) After a while there is a junction where six paths come together at a hillside spring and seat. Here the route continues straight ahead as before but is now signposted as the higher path to Hurlstone Point.
   In summertime the surrounding trees are all-enveloping, so it is not possible to measure the height gained until the open ground at the spring is reached. The view from here shows the fertile Vale of Porlock climbing to high, wild hills with a glimpse of the sea on the right.

(6) The path eventually veers into Lynch Combe, the first of two short, steep valleys set into the side of the plateau. Ahead a rising moorland ridge marks the walk's one major climb. This starts beyond the first combe.

(7) Passing through the two gates in the bottom of Lynch Combe, the route follows the left branch at a fork, the steep path up the valley bottom being ignored. The way forward is now gently upwards through trees, heading back in the general direction of Porlock Bay.

(8) At the end of the hillside the path turns right and emerges onto the side of Church Combe, the next valley.
   Massed trees, the major feature of the walk so far, have now come to an end. A wayside seat is provided here for those wishing to enjoy the view, which embraces Church Combe's steep opposite bank, the sea and the coast receding into the west.

(9) This is a turning point of the walk. To the right of the seat, an unsignposted, rough path heads steeply uphill. This most inauspicious start to the most spectacular section of the walk soon leads to an airy clamber up a ridge. From here the ground drops away into Church Combe on the left, Lynch Combe on the right and Porlock Vale behind.
   The path is now clear-cut, climbing over short heather, grass and, in places,

The hills traversed in Walks 8 and 9, with Hurlstone Combe on the left

the exposed rock of the ridge. On clear days the views defy description, presenting as glorious a combination of land and sea as anyone could wish for.

(10) The climb becomes easier as height is gained. Trees come into view along the skyline on the right and these mark the next objective. On approaching the top of the moor, the path joins and leaves other tracks and paths as it winds around the shallow head of Lynch Combe. For part of the way there are old earthworks on the right dating from the war. The skyline trees can now be seen to mark the car park at the end of the road across the moor.

(11) On approaching the car park, the walk crosses the road onto a track heading left and eastwards, parallel to the highway and in front of a plantation of trees. From here, with only one minor deviation, the track continues for approximately a quarter of a mile to the prominent stone hut erected as an Acland family memorial in the nineteenth century.

The memorial has two outstanding features: solid stone construction and inscriptions of sentimental religious Victorian poetry, nowadays very much out of favour.

From this spot nearby Selworthy Beacon appears a modest rise, very different from the impressive summit seen from a distance.

Church and Lynch Combes

(12) The next port of call is Bury Castle. The route heads to the south-west from the side of the Hut displaying part of a poem by Keble, and at an acute angle to the approach from the car park. The walk goes along a gentle downhill track bordered by trees.

Soon the route swings to the south across a broad, near-level spur clad in gorse, bracken, heather and graceful silver birches. This lovely parkland contrasts with both the high bleak moorland above and the steep, thickly wooded slopes below.

(13) The way forward across this demi-paradise is along a track which bears left at a fork and signposted to Bury Castle. On arrival, the walk follows a path straight through the site, ignoring another on the right.

These earthworks, perched on the end of the ridge, are an impressive sight but difficult to interpret. Although 'Bury' is a variant of the Anglo-Saxon word *burgh*, meaning 'a fortified place', this is an Iron Age structure. It may have remained in use until the Dark Ages, but nobody knows for sure. Archaeological work has yet to be carried out on the site. Today the scene provides a puzzle for the visitor, rough grazing for farm animals and a home for wild rabbits.

The Dunkery range from Bury Castle

(14) Selworthy, the next objective, lies downhill to the left in a south-easterly direction. The intervening steep slope is covered with mature trees and visibility, especially in summer, is limited. Consequently the way forward is not always clear.

The best solution is to turn right, away from the path which has passed through the centre of the site and then, at a T-junction, left onto another. This leads down into the trees. From here a succession of zigzag paths should be followed in a downhill direction. On approaching the bottom of the slope, the walker will be to the west of the village and should therefore turn left to reach it. (Although this description may sound rather vague, the village will be hard to miss.)

(15) Selworthy Green is entered from above. The tea garden lies below and the way out is uphill, past the shop and War Memorial. From here the walk proceeds in front of the church along the lane to the east.

The narrow highway is deep and bordered by hedges, but gaps present a splendid panorama of the fields of the upper Vale of Porlock climbing to wooded hills crowned by Dunkery Beacon.

(16) The lane is followed for three-quarters of a mile, ignoring the bridleway on the right down to Headon Cross which was followed in Walk 4. The lane turns right in front of Little Headon Plantation and here the walk takes the footpath following the original line of the lane, entry being gained over a stile.

(17) This footpath goes eastwards along the top of a long meadow bordering the north side of the wood.

Below, the two surviving old settlements of the area, Hindon and Wydon, nestle into clefts on the opposite side of the valley, their meadows climbing to bleak, windswept tops. This farming scene contrasts with the woods and moors of the earlier part of the walk.

From here a glimpse of the sea to the east indicates that Minehead is not far away.

(18) Continuing eastwards, the path eventually enters Little Headon Plantation for a short distance before emerging onto the left side of a meadow rising to the right.

(19) Having followed the left boundary of this field for 400 yards, the walk turns left through a field gate and heads downhill along the right side of another field to a lane in the bottom of the valley.

Minehead, still invisible at this point, sits in the lower reaches of this valley, less than a mile away.

(20) The route now turns right along the tarmac towards a group of Scots pines near Bratton Court. Here it takes a left turn through a gate beside a rubbish dump to enter a hedge-enclosed track heading towards a tree-covered hillside.

(21) Passing through a metal field gate into the trees, the walk turns right along the bottom of the woodland. After a quarter of a mile, this path turns downhill across two stiles in close succession into a meadow and then heads half left across the centre to another stile on the opposite side. From here the path proceeds along the left side of another, smaller meadow to join a track. This passes to the left and below a miscellany of buildings before entering a tarmac lane.

(22) Here the route turns right and along the backs of some of Woodcombe's homes before veering left at a road junction.

(23) Almost immediately opposite and uphill there is a footpath sign pointing to North Hill. This is the way to go. After passing along a private drive in front of two bungalows, the entrance to the footpath can be found on the left. Thirty yards ahead there is a hand gate. A climb towards wild slopes follows.

(24) On reaching two paths across the face of the hill, the route turns right, taking the lower path, and then winds gently down the slope for the next third of a mile. All other side turnings should be ignored.

Although the route is still surrounded by trees and masses of wild buddleia, the sounds of urban traffic now penetrate from below.

(25) The path eventually emerges onto Whitecross Lane and the way forward is to the left for 200 yards before turning right down Whitecross Way, a short, steep cul-de-sac. Houses now stand on all sides.

(26) The cul-de-sac soon dwindles to a tarmac track and then to an unsurfaced one. Here the route continues downhill, ignoring the tarmac path straight ahead.

(27) At the bottom there is a left turn onto Parks Lane. This is followed over a crossroads to Watery Lane, where a right turn leads back to the town centre.

———◆———

⇥ WALK 10 ⇤

ALONG THE SHORE
FROM WATCHET TO MINEHEAD

*This may not be a true Exmoor walk, but its delights add a new dimension
to the wider Exmoor scene. The route follows the predominantly lonely and
peaceful shore between the two towns – and there are no hills to climb! Along the
way the scene changes from eroded rock platforms beneath stark cliffs to wide
sandy beaches backed by a low-lying coast. Eight miles and four hours of steady
walking.*

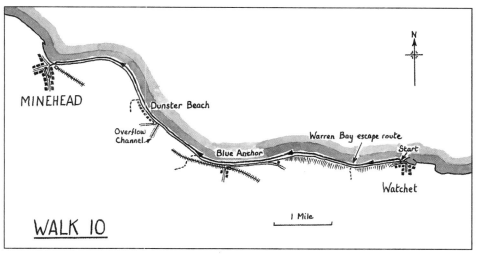

WALK 10

IMPORTANT POINTS TO NOTE BEFORE STARTING OUT

* For the two miles between Watchet and Blue Anchor the sea covers the foot
  of the cliffs at high tide and the only escape route is at Warren Bay. Safety is
  a priority and the walk should only be tackled two to three hours after high
  tide. Tide tables should be consulted beforehand.

* Good walking boots are recommended for all the walks in this book and
  especially for this one. The eroded rock platforms along a substantial part of
  the way are very uneven and can be treacherously slippery without proper
  footwear. This is definitely not a walk for beach sandals.

(1) Watchet is reached by train or bus from Minehead.

On alighting it is well worth while spending some time looking around this fascinating old seaport. Watchet was an Anglo-Saxon burgh with its own mint and first came into recorded history as a place raided more than once by the Danes.

Although some older buildings remain, much of the present town dates from the nineteenth century, when Watchet shipped high-grade iron ore mined in the Brendon Hills. It remained a working port until recent times.

Over a long period the town's men and vessels ranged far afield. During the nineteenth century one of its most famous sons, John Short, otherwise known as Yankee Jack, helped to break the blockade of the southern states during the American Civil War. In the early years of the twentieth century he sang many shanties and other songs, including 'Rio Grande' and 'Shenandoah', to Cecil Sharp, the folk-song collector.

It was also from Watchet that the Ancient Mariner, poetry's most famous sailor, set sail. His fictitious meeting with the wedding guest at the beginning of the poem is set in the churchyard high above the town.

For more information on this fascinating old port, a visit should be made to the little museum below the mariners' chapel in Market Street.

(2) Starting from the harbour slipway, the walk heads westwards into West Street. At the end of the first row of terraced houses on the right, a gap marks the entrance to a concrete ramp down to the stony beach.

In former times Watchet was sheltered by headlands on each side, but these have long since been worn away and the town is now exposed to the sea. Following recent storm damage, a tall concrete wall was added to protect part of the waterfront.

(3) The stones of the beach are unpleasant to walk on; the eroded rock platforms further to the west provide a better surface. The route follows these around the remains of a headland.

Across the water can be seen the destination of the walk: distant Minehead and its imposing headland.

(4) Ahead the large stretches of soft sand exposed at low tide make heavy going. Firmer ground can often be found on the sand adjacent to the stony upper shore. Down towards the sea, the sand gives way to thick, unpleasant mud.

Substantial cliff falls have occurred here in recent times, leaving random piles of huge boulders as impressive reminders of the powers of nature.

(5) The final part of the sandy reach is low-lying, and if the walk is attempted too soon after high tide, it will be necessary to wait for the sea to recede from the bottom of the cliff.

(6) Ahead lies Warren Bay, which is a modest indentation rather than a true inlet. The two access points at the top of the beach offer the only means of escape from the shore between here and Blue Anchor Bay, well over a mile away.

This coast is composed of softer, younger rocks than those of Exmoor to the west and is well known for fossils of all sizes, including ammonites. The most productive area for fossil-hunting on this walk is the quarter-mile stretch to the west of Warren Bay. However, both time and patience are needed for success.

(7) The way forward is over a mix of loose stones and eroded rock platforms. The green seaweed clinging to the rock on the wetter reaches of the shore can be very slippery and requires careful negotiation.

The cliff strata are contorted into fantastic curving shapes nearby, but soon become almost as straight and level as they were when laid down as sediment on the seabed millions of years ago.

(8) Further along, beneath undercut cliffs, a firm bed of small pebbles provides a suitable path.

The walk now passes through what seems like a lost world. Rugged cliffs stand above and fantastic sea-carved rock platforms slope down to the waters below. Here the only reminders of humanity are views of distant Minehead and Welsh towns and factories across the sea.

The grey cliffs here contain prominent layers of alabaster, varying in colour from near-white to orange-pink. In the past it was used to make ornaments, and a stone picked up on this beach makes an attractive paperweight.

(9) On rounding the coast, a recent massive rock fall comes into view. This has left huge blocks of stone weighing hundreds of tons scattered on the shore like abandoned playthings.

Distant reaches of the coast to the west are now in view, commencing with nearby Blue Anchor Bay.

The cliffs have not yet ended, but the grey lias rock which was predominant earlier suddenly gives way to a less substantial red sandstone, the source of the brown sand underfoot.

(10) At first stretches of this sand alternate with rock platforms heading diagonally down the beach. The former is more pleasant to walk on and there is a tendency to follow it down the shore, but beware: thick mud lurks there!

Blue Anchor is notable for its fine sandy beach and a promenade three-quarters of a mile long, built as a sea defence. There is a public house at the east end, toilets in the middle and a café near the railway station at the west end.

(11) Beyond Blue Anchor the walk continues along the beach, passing low-lying coastal fields bordered by the railway.

Along this stretch there is only a puny shingle bank to protect the land from the sea. As the beach swings round to the north-west, views open up across meadows to Dunster Castle, backed by high, dark hills: a fairy-tale scene. The railway is now inland. The eye, constantly drawn seawards, is caught by old wooden sea defences sculpted by the waves into fantastic shapes.

(12) The next landmark is the River Avill overflow channel outfall. Although often dry in summer, in winter it can become a raging torrent, plunging onto the beach in cascades of white water.

When dry, the outfall can be crossed, but if necessary, the bridge a short distance inland may be used. Dunster Beach car park lies on the other side. Public toilets and light refreshments are available here during the summer months.

(13) The way ahead is now along a public footpath in front of a long line of wooden beach chalets.

These chalets, a relic of the seaside holiday boom of the inter-war years, remain very popular. Many are owned or rented by city-dwellers who come here year after year to enjoy the peace and quiet of the place.

(14) After the chalets there is an outfall onto the beach and two World War Two pillboxes faced with rounded beach stones. The remainder of the walk follows part of the route taken in Walk 5. There is now a choice between walking across the beach or along the public footpath on top of the bank. The sand is usually firm, allowing the walker to make steady, fast progress while remaining absorbed in the seascape.

(15) On the preferred beach route there are no views of Minehead and its massive headland above the sea until after the scrub-covered shingle bank at Warren Point. From here the railway station close to the town centre is soon reached.

→ WALK 11 ←

A LONG WALK THROUGH WOODS AND SECRET PLACES

This walk passes through remote forests and along a secluded wild valley. Starting from Dunster, it takers the walker to Bonniton, Long Combe, Nurcott Farm, Croydon House, Timberscombe, Sloe Combe and Hopcott before returning to Minehead. The path along the valley bottom between Nurcott Farm and Croydon House is rough underfoot and good walking boots are essential. All the paths and tracks are signposted and often have blue, yellow or red waymarks. The route is undulating and there are two high hills to climb. Eleven miles and six to seven hours of steady walking.

(1) The outing begins with a journey on the No. 39 bus from Minehead to the terminus at the Foresters Arms in Dunster.

(2) The walk commences down the side lane leading to the edge of the village at Gallox Bridge.

(3) After crossing the bridge and passing thatched cottages on the right, the route takes the second of two turnings to the right, a well-used track climbing steadily through woodland.

As height is gained there are glimpses of massed trees clinging to the opposite side of the Avill Valley. Most of the walk lies within the basin of this small, lively river.

At the start, people may be seen out with their dogs, but such sightings will become increasingly rare.

(4) A track on the left leading uphill through a gate should be ignored. At a fork further along, the route takes the left branch. A second turning to the right at a T-junction heading for a viewpoint, and a track approaching diagonally from the left should also be ignored.

Finally, at a meeting of four tracks the walk turns right and downhill to approach but not join the tarmac lane in the valley bottom at Bonniton. The way ahead is now along a well-used track on the left. This heads up the left side of a long narrow meadow in the valley bottom. Conifers cover the hillside on the

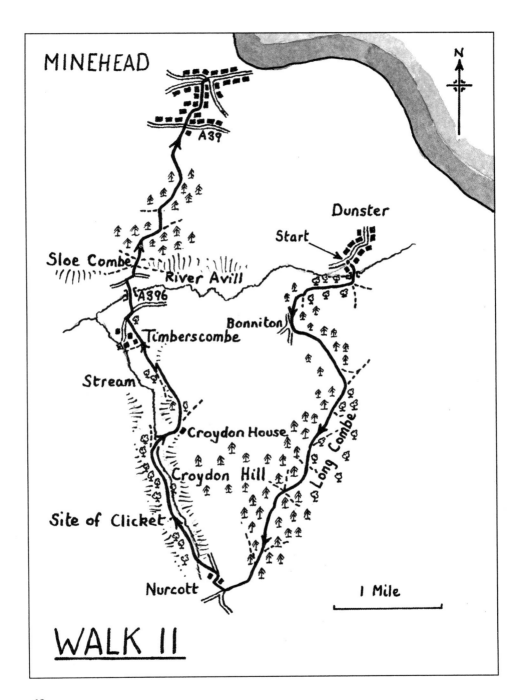

MINEHEAD

Dunster

Start

Sloe Combe

River Avill

A39

A396

Bonniton

Timberscombe

Stream

Croydon House

Long Combe

Croydon Hill

Site of Clicket

Nurcott

N

1 Mile

WALK 11

left and there are two small quarries along the way. A track joining at an acute angle from the left should be ignored.

The name 'Bonniton' might suggest a village, but there is none here. It is believed to derive from a former bonding toll house. (Perhaps tolls were levied here on flocks climbing to the rough pasture on the surrounding, now wooded, hills.)

(5) The long meadow in the valley bottom ends after half a mile. The route veers right and downhill at a fork and right again at a T-junction.

(6) A quarter of a mile further on there is a meeting of ways, where the most heavily used branch heads left. The walk continues straight ahead into Long Combe along a track designated as a footpath.

Long Combe is, as its name suggests, a long valley, and the climb through it to the top of the high hill ahead is gentle. This is a secret place. Regimented conifers march down the steep slope on the right and native oaks cling to the high bank on the left. A stream rushes down the narrow bottom, allowing barely enough room for the track. The two jostle and cross more than once and fording the water can be difficult at times.

(7) The next landmark is another meeting of ways. Here one prominent track approaches down the valley left bank and another from the right. The route of the walk continues up the steepening valley bottom and turns into a path.

This path quickly becomes rough and the increasingly untamed scenery all around gives the impression of untrodden wilderness ahead. Then, ever more obscure, the route climbs away through trees to the right of the valley head.

(8) All doubts are suddenly removed as the walker emerges onto a broad forest track. Here the route turns left, crossing near-level terrain covered in massed conifers. At the next meeting of tracks the route turns right and immediately left, continuing in the same general direction as before.

(9) A quarter of a mile further on, close to the 370-metre-high summit of the walk, another cross track will be seen. This should be ignored.

(10) During the ensuing gradual descent there are glimpses of more open country on the right. A further cross track and another filtering in from the right should both be ignored. It is now clear that the woods are coming to an end.

(11) At the final track junction near the last of the trees, the route veers right and downhill along a well-used track to a road junction and turns right down a lane.

Long Combe

This high, lonely country is the southernmost point of the walk. Here attractive, hedge-enclosed meadows, divided by occasional steep valleys, roll on and away to distant hills.

(12) The road twists to the right past Nurcott Farm, with its striking monkey-puzzle tree, and then left at Baker's Farm, where a signposted downhill track on the left marks the next stage of the walk. For the next mile and a half the path is rough underfoot.

This valley bottom, once inhabited and exploited by man, has reverted almost to wilderness. The ruined remains of houses, a lime kiln and extensive quarry workings bear witness to the past.

(13) Scrub alternates with ragged spinneys as the often ill-defined path weaves along the left bank of the watercourse. Here yellow waymarks painted on trees and posts provide a welcome guide. Along the way the route passes a ruined building of the lost hamlet of Clicket.

(14) There are two footpaths signposted to Croydon Hill on the right. The first should be ignored, but the second, half a mile beyond the first, should not. Beyond a steep meadow and after crossing a small side stream, the walker will find a footbridge over the main stream and a signpost. Once the stream is crossed, the delightful lost-world valley bottom is left behind.

(15) The walk then follows a muddy track with yellow waymarks. After it has climbed and veered to the right, these marks unexpectedly point through a gate into a rough meadow on the left. The route then turns right, following the top of this meadow with the track immediately above. There is a waymarked hand gate ahead, and after this the path drops down to a small stream before climbing to join the farm track from Croydon House. From here the nearby farm buildings, but not the house, can be seen on the right.

The reason for the unexpected diversion is now obvious. The public footpath has been rerouted around the farm buildings.

(16) The walk turns left along the farm track and at the next fork veers right up another ascending side track through trees. The first bridleway entrance on the left should be ignored, but after a modest climb to the end of a small wood the second, also on the left, is entered through a gate.

The next section is delightful, following the lip of a heather- and gorse-covered bank below large meadows. After miles of intimate scenery, there is now a wide panorama embracing many distant hills, including, in centre stage, the glorious heather-covered slopes of the Dunkery range.

(17) After half a mile a gate appears. Immediately in front of this the bridleway turns left and zigzags down the hill to turn right onto the vehicle track from Croydon House. The buildings of Timberscombe can now be seen directly ahead.

(18) After passing a disused quarry on the right the track reaches a group of dwellings. Here the route is along a footpath immediately to the right of an old house with bay windows facing the line of approach. The new path follows the same northerly direction as before.

The centre of Timberscombe is now close by, and if refreshments are needed there is a public house here.

(19) The new path, through trees and scrub, climbs and then levels out above old enclosures on the left. After 400 yards a small meadow with a wooden stable-block appears through a gap on the left. The path turns through this gap and then right across two stiles in succession to reach two adjacent low fences without stiles on the lower side of the meadow.

(20) From here the way forward is down to and across a track from the stables.

Then the walk continues to the right , taking a less obvious downhill path that goes through a cluster of bushes below.

Beware: the next path junction – with the main road – is extremely dangerous! This path emerges from bushes directly onto a narrow and blind bend of the often busy A396. There is no footway.

(21) The walk turns right and proceeds along the road for 200 yards before turning left down a lane signposted to Wootton Courtney. The keen eye will note the incorrect spelling!

(22) The lane is followed for a quarter of a mile across the valley bottom, passing over the River Avill. The walk then turns right at the next T-junction and, 200 yards further on, left onto a signposted track heading uphill.

There is a long, high ridge between here and Minehead. This is crossed by an old packhorse route leading from the interior of Exmoor to Minehead harbour.

(23) The increasing height brings extensive views. On reaching a fork at the entrance to lovely winding Sloe Combe, the walk veers left and uphill. This track curves and ascends. Later it crosses another passing along the wooded side of the hill.

(24) Eventually the prominent near-level ridge track is reached. Crossing over and passing a small grassy area with a picnic bench on the right, the route continues downhill along a track signposted to Minehead.

Although the town is now close by, few people will be seen up here.

(25) During the descent the route veers left at a fork above a woodland clearing and then re-enters trees, soon joining the top of the tarmac lane above Higher Hopcott.

(26) This lane continues down to the A39. After crossing the main road, the route follows the now-familiar footpath between dwellings down to Poundfield Road, where right and left turns into Bampton Street lead to the town centre.

→ WALK 12 ←

FROM EXFORD TO MINEHEAD
OVER THE TOP OF DUNKERY

Starting from Exford, the walk goes to Rowbarrows, Dunkery Beacon, Brockwell, Wootton Courtenay, Wootton Common and Periton back to Minehead. This is the last walk of the series and it incorporates a lofty passage along the Dunkery ridge. Paradoxically, the second and lesser climb of the walk is more demanding than the first. Much of the route is over high moors and may not be suitable for poor weather conditions. Eleven miles and a full day's walk.

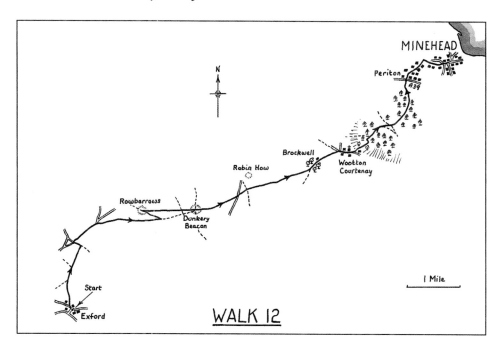

WALK 12

(1) The expedition begins with a journey on the No. 285 bus (summer only) from Minehead to Exford.

Exford may surprise the first-time visitor. Although at the impressive height of 280 metres above sea-level, it is not an old, raw upland settlement on high moors but a relatively modern village surrounded by rolling meadows and trees.

The village has shops, hotels and tearooms. There are also public toilets beside the filling-station.

(2) The walk commences along Porlock Road with the village green-cum-football pitch on the left.

(3) After 200 yards the route turns right up Coombe Lane, a cul-de-sac. Dwellings are soon left behind as the way wanders uphill beside hedge-bordered meadows. All other paths and tracks to both left and right should be ignored.

The ground rises gently for over a mile, the scene changing subtly until the lane has become a bridleway, a rough track crossing large, exposed meadows. A new feature has appeared: the summit cairn of Dunkery Beacon, standing at only a modest height above the immediate surroundings. For those who are more familiar with the wild, tall sides of the Dunkery range facing north, this may come as the second surprise of the day. The fields rising northwards from Exford reach the exceptional height of 480 metres above sea-level. The south-facing slopes on this side of the hill are gentler and sunnier.

(4) On reaching the top of the fields, the bridleway turns left into an arching avenue of trees. These are formed from overgrown beech hedges on top of earthen boundary banks.

(5) Two hundred yards ahead, the avenue reaches a junction of tarmac roads on the edge of open moorland. Here the walk turns right onto the highway and heads north-east.

This lovely open heather moorland, stretching far to the north, is owned by the National Trust. Its first sighting is always a great pleasure, evoking a wonderful sense of freedom.

(6) The route continues for half a mile along the lane, flanked by the moor on the left and a beech hedge on the right. At the next road fork it turns right and eastwards along a rough track. The open moorland on the left has now begun to rise but the ragged beech hedge on the right still borders farmland.

(7) After half a mile the modest rise on the left has become Rowbarrows at the western end of the Dunkery range, looking very different from its northern view.

(8) This hilltop can be reached by a short, steep scramble up through the heather, but there is a better approach further along the track.

(9) At the point where the track shifts distinctly to the right and the summit cairn of Dunkery Beacon comes into view directly ahead, there is a path on the left. This heads back at an oblique angle through the heather to the summit of Rowbarrows.

The flattish top of Rowbarrows is marked by the stony remains of Bronze Age burial mounds and very little else. The wide views to the north may be rewarding, but it is the nearby summit of Dunkery Beacon which dominates and draws the walker on.

(10) The path along the broad ridge between the two summits is clear-cut, but its surface is rough. Nevertheless the top of the Beacon soon looms above and a short climb leads to scattered stones and the large summit cairn. This commemorates the donation of the hill to the nation by several local landowners. The ground here has become eroded by horses' hooves and human feet and is best avoided.

From this 500-metre summit there are splendid all-round views. Heather moors beckon northwards to Porlock Bay, Selworthy Beacon and beyond the sea to the Welsh coast and mountains. To the south the land drops to the rolling farmland of mid-Devon backed by the hills and tors of Dartmoor.

Dunkery's name is derived from a combination of the Celtic words *dun*, meaning 'hill' and *creagh*', rough and rocky ground'. The latter is most familiar in the form of the modern word 'crag'. More rock can be seen on Dunkery than on other Exmoor summits, but it is not extensive.

The summit was used as a fire beacon for hundreds of years, and human activity over a long period has all but obliterated the Bronze Age burial mounds which once stood on this site.

Solitude is a rare commodity here as the top and the path down to the east are much frequented by visitors who park their vehicles along the road below.

(11) The path makes a slow steady descent to the road and then heads downhill along a clear-cut path below Robin How at the eastern end of the Dunkery range. The side path to this high point should be ignored. Beyond the road most signs of humanity are left behind.

The white and cream buildings of Wootton Courtenay, backed by the steep wooded hillside of Wootton Common, have come into view directly ahead. Both the village and the Common are on the route of the walk, the latter representing the second major climb of the day.

(12) During the descent, heather gives way to bracken, prickly gorse, bushes and finally trees.

The bottom of the slope was a source of high-grade iron ore in the nineteenth century and evidence of this activity still remains in the rich red soil and the occasional lumps of heavy brown-red ore beside the way.

(13) From Brockwell to Wootton Courtenay the walk follows the lane used on an earlier walk. This time, however, after turning right onto the road through the village, Roadway Lane is ignored.

(14) The walk continues through the village centre, passing both shop and church on the left.

Wootton Courtenay, a warm, sunny spot below the heights of Wootton Common, is a mix of old buildings in keeping with their surroundings and modern residences that would look more at home in the outer-London suburbs.

(15) After a sharp bend in the road a small vineyard appears on the left, next to a steep meadow. The walker should enter the meadow over a stile and climb to another stile on the edge of trees high above.

(16) The upward progress continues, ignoring all other tempting tracks and paths to left and right. Finally, above the remains of old hilly enclosures, the climb reaches an area recently cleared and replanted with trees. Here the uphill slope eases.

With increased height and more open surroundings, there are now wide views over the Avill Valley to the village of Timberscombe and the extensive woods of Croydon Hill beyond.

(17) A track joining at an acute angle on the left should be ignored. Shortly afterwards the familiar, well-used track along the top of the ridge is reached. This is followed to the right for a few yards before turning left and downhill through scrubland along a path signposted to Periton.

In marked contrast with the popular top of Dunkery Beacon, few people will be found up here.

(18) As the way ahead is not always obvious, it may be helpful to bear in mind that Minehead lies to the north and downhill. Soon gaps in trees on the left reveal lovely views of the steep wooded sides of Periton Combe below.

(19) The well-worn path continues to descend close to open ground on the right before making a modest climb over the top of Hopcott Brake.

(20) A steep descent down the side of woodland leads to the small stream and the main track in the bottom of Periton Combe, close to the A39.

(21) From here the remainder of the route is the same as that followed in Walk 7. It crosses the main road and traverses the deep, tree-enclosed section of Periton Lane.

(22) At the end of the lane, Hillview Road is followed down to Parks Walk on the right.

(23) The Parks Walk ends on Parkhouse Road, where a left turn leads back to the town centre.

—◄■►—

AFTERWORD

A 21-MILE WALK ALONG
THE GLORIOUS EXMOOR COAST

If you have completed the other walks in this guidebook, you may like to consider an unforgettable challenge (provided you are fit enough): the 21-mile-walk along the South West Coast Path from Minehead to Lynmouth.

The unique feature of this lonely, unspoilt coast is a line of high hogsback hills falling steeply to the sea. It is broken in only one place, at the Vale of Porlock. Elsewhere between these heights small noisy streams tumble on to rocky beaches, once the haunt of smugglers.

The scenic delights are ever-changing. Beyond the trees close to Minehead there are the high open moors above the sea crowned by Selworthy Beacon. A steep descent past the scree-covered sides of Hurlstone Combe leads to the lush chequerboard fields of the Vale of Porlock, famed for the quality of their malting barley. Beyond Porlock and its Vale there is a lofty winding path through trees above the sea to Culbone.

Culbone, once the isolated home of leprosy sufferers, consists of just two dwellings and a tiny ancient church and there is no road leading down to it. The recently diverted walk then passes along a shelf of high farmland perched between the moors on one side and the steep wooded slopes down to the sea on the other. It was here, probably at Ash Farm, that Coleridge first penned the lines of his famous incomplete poem 'Kubla Khan'.

Back down among the steep tree-covered slopes, the route leads through Glenthorne, a romantic estate of great beauty, both natural and man-made, created by a wealthy gentleman of the cloth in the early part of the nineteenth century. The county boundary between Somerset and Devon is crossed at the Sisters' Fountain, a rather dismal, obscure nook marked a stone cross surmounting a cairn.

Afterwards the South West Coast Path again winds through more trees above the sea up to the massive bulk of the Foreland, a headland visible for many miles back along the route. Here the estuarial waters of the Bristol Channel begin to merge into the broad Atlantic.

At long last the destination comes into view, the mountainous setting of Lynmouth and Lynton, plunging down to the sea forming a dramatic scene. Close at hand the weather-battered tower of Countisbury Church peeps above the minimal protection provided by the adjacent hillside. From here the route is downhill all the rest of the way, passing across a steep bare slope below the massive Iron Age fortress of Wind Hill.

Much of the route between Minehead and Lynmouth goes through lonely country, but there are facilities for walkers at Bossington (tea gardens and toilets); Porlock (full facilities); Porlock Weir (café, pub and toilets); Culbone (do-it-yourself café only), and Countisbury (pub). Lynmouth has a full range of cafés, shops, hotels and pubs. However, the facilities at all these places can be very limited out of season. It is probably advisable to take along a packed meal, together with plenty to drink, particularly if the weather is hot.

It should be emphasized that this is a long walk, characterized by continuous ups and downs. By maintaining a fast pace it is possible to cover the distance in seven to eight hours, but it is better to allow ten hours. This will allow the constantly changing and often spectacular scenery along the way to be enjoyed to the full.

There is a limited bus service between Lynmouth and Minehead (No. 300 Route). Timetables are subject to alteration and it is essential to check before embarking on the walk. Assuming a return to Minehead on the early evening (and last!) bus from Lynmouth is planned, it will be necessary to start out from Minehead at around 7 a.m. – a most rewarding time to be abroad on a lovely summer's day.

The South West Coast Path is well signposted and provided walkers keep their eyes open there is very little chance of becoming lost. However, a map is always helpful, not only to check one's progress but also if tiredness, blisters or lack of time make it necessary to leave the Coast Path and divert inland to the main coast road, the A39.